D1712512

math standards workout

COMPUTATION
SKILLS

50 MATH SUPER PUZZLES

By Thomas Canavan

rosen publishing's
rosen
central

This edition first published in 2012 by The Rosen Publishing Group, Inc.
29 East 21st Street, New York, NY 10010

Author: Thomas Canavan
Editor: Joe Harris
Design: Jane Hawkins
Cover design: Jane Hawkins

Library of Congress Cataloging-in-Publication Data

Canavan, Thomas.
Computation skills : 50 math super puzzles / Thomas Canavan.
p. cm. — (Math standards workout)
Includes bibliographical references and index.
ISBN 978-1-4488-6673-1 (library binding) — ISBN 978-1-4488-6680-9 (pbk.) — ISBN 978-1-4488-6686-1 (6-pack)
1. Arithmetic—Juvenile literature. 2. Mathematical recreations—Juvenile literature. I. Title.
QA107.2.C34 2012
513—dc23
2011028570

Printed in China
SL002073US

CPSIA Compliance Information: Batch #W12YA. For further information, contact Rosen Publishing, New York, New York, at 1-800-237-9932.

Contents

Introduction

Why do you need this book?

How do you feel after soccer or basketball practice? You probably feel that your weakest skills improved—and your real talents got that much better. Math problem-solving is just the same. The puzzles in this book will exercise the different math skills involved in computation. They will help you to build on your strengths and improve in those areas where you are weakest.

How will this book help you at school?

Computation Skills complements the National Council of Teachers of Mathematics (NCTM) framework of Math Standards, providing an engaging enhancement of the curriculum in the following areas:

> *Number and Operations Standard: Compute Fluently*
> *Number and Operations Standard: Understand the Meanings of Operations and How They Interrelate*

Why have we chosen these puzzles?

This *Math Standards Workout* title features a range of interesting and absorbing puzzle types, challenging students to master the following skills to arrive at solutions:

• Develop fluency with basic number combinations for multiplication and division: e.g. Pyramid Plus, Number Crunch, Total Concentration

• Identify and use relationships between operations, such as division as the inverse of multiplication, to solve problems: e.g What's the Number?, One to Nine

• Develop fluency in adding, subtracting, multiplying, and dividing whole numbers: e.g. Symbol Math, Circling In

NOTE TO READERS

If you have borrowed this book from a school or classroom library, please respect other students and DO NOT write your answers in the book. Always write your answers on a separate sheet of paper.

One to Nine

Using the numbers one to nine, complete these six equations (three reading across and three reading downward). Every number is used once only, and one is already in place. Write your answers on a separate sheet of paper.

1

$1 \quad 2 \quad 3 \quad 4 \quad 5 \quad 6 \quad 7 \quad 8 \quad 9$

	x		−		=	15
+		x		+		
	−		x	3	=	21
−		+		x		
	x		+		=	17
=		=		=		
10		11		84		

Making Arrangements

Arrange one each of the four numbers below, as well as one each of the symbols x (times), – (minus), and + (plus) in every row and column. You should arrive at the answer at the end of the row or column, making the calculations in the order in which they appear. Some are already in place. Write your answers on a separate sheet of paper.

2 3 7 8

3	+	8	x	2	–	7	=	15
						+		
							=	48
		+						
							=	24
		2					=	12
=		=		=		=		
64		8		33		27		

What's the Number?

In the diagram below, what number should replace the question mark?
Write your answer on a separate sheet of paper.

3

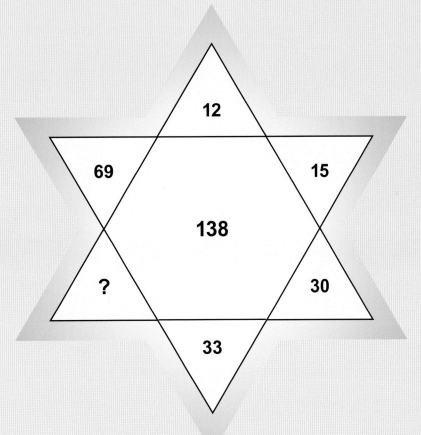

Circling In

The three empty circles should contain the symbols +, − , and x in some order, to make a series that leads to the number in the middle. Each symbol must be used once and calculations are made in a clockwise direction. Write your answers on a separate sheet of paper.

4

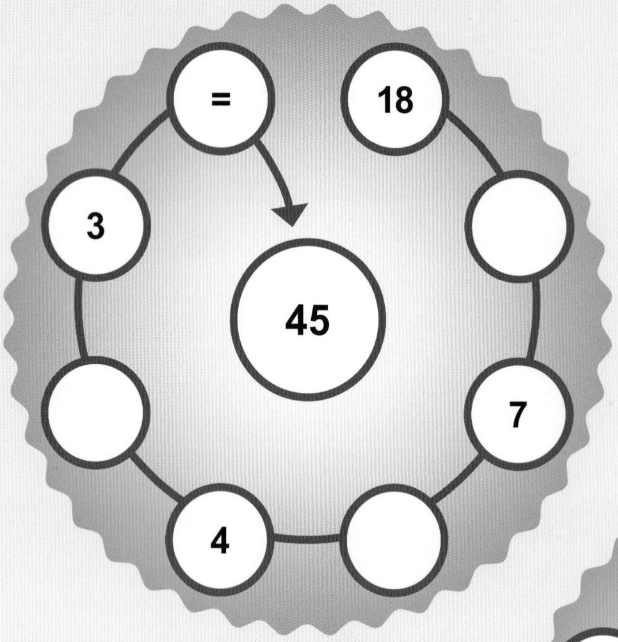

= 18

3

45

7

4

5

= 11

17

83

9

1

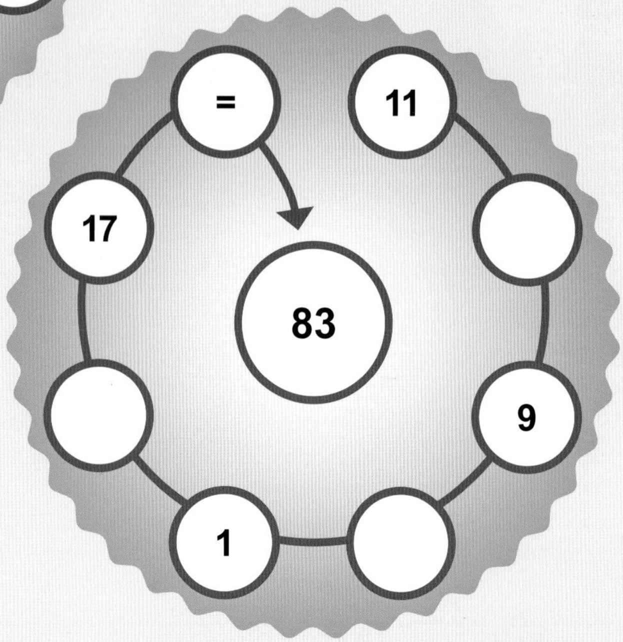

Pyramid Plus

The number in each circle is the sum of the two numbers below it. Just work out the missing numbers in every circle! Write your answers on a separate sheet of paper.

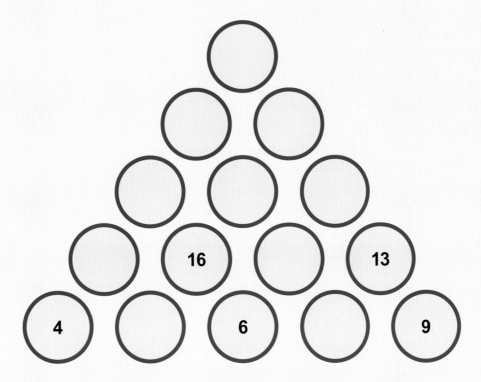

One to Nine

Using the numbers one to nine, complete these six equations (three reading across and three reading downward). Every number is used once only, and one is already in place. Write your answers on a separate sheet of paper.

7

1 2 3 4 5 6 7 8 9

	−		x		=	8
+		x		+		
1	+		x		=	36
x		+		x		
	x		−		=	33
=		=		=		
45		25		26		

Total Concentration

The blank squares below should contain whole numbers between 1 and 30 inclusive, any of which may occur more than once, or not at all. The numbers in every horizontal row add up to the totals on the right, as do the two long diagonal lines extending from corner to corner; those in every vertical column add up to the totals along the bottom. Write your answers on a separate sheet of paper.

							119
22		1	18	23	6		121
24			27	16	24	15	138
	17	22	11	3	20		110
23	4	29			9	22	132
25	1		2	29		26	127
8	26	14	18	25		27	128
	13	19		5	19	21	100
121	103	121	104	129	116	162	133

Symbol Math

Each symbol stands for a different number. In order to reach the correct total at the end of each row and column, what is the value of the circle, pentagon, square, and star? Write your answers on a separate sheet of paper.

9

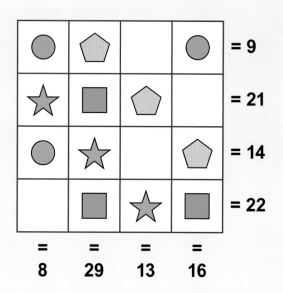

Number Crunch

Starting at the top left with the number provided, work down from one box to another, applying the mathematical instructions to your running total. Write your answers on a separate sheet of paper.

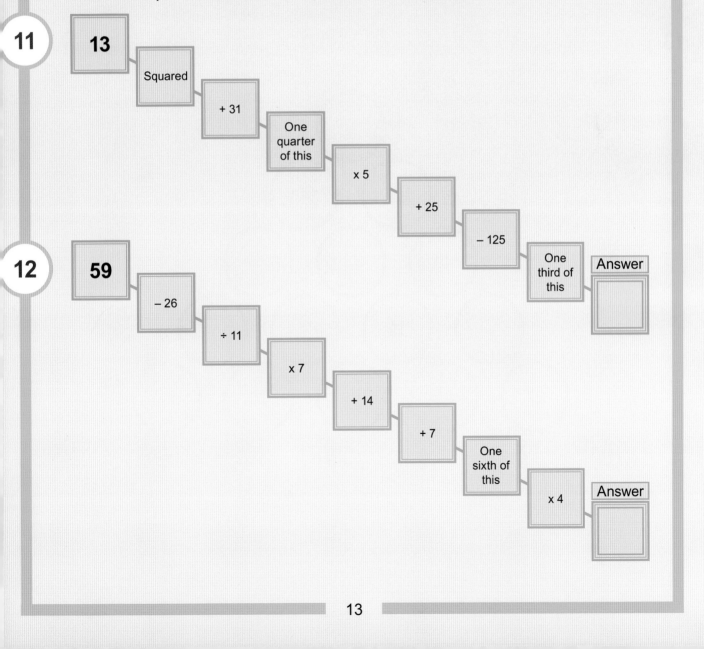

11

13
Squared
+ 31
One quarter of this
x 5
+ 25
− 125
One third of this
Answer

12

59
− 26
÷ 11
x 7
+ 14
+ 7
One sixth of this
x 4
Answer

Pyramid Plus

The number in each circle is the sum of the two numbers below it. Just work out the missing numbers in every circle! Write your answers on a separate sheet of paper.

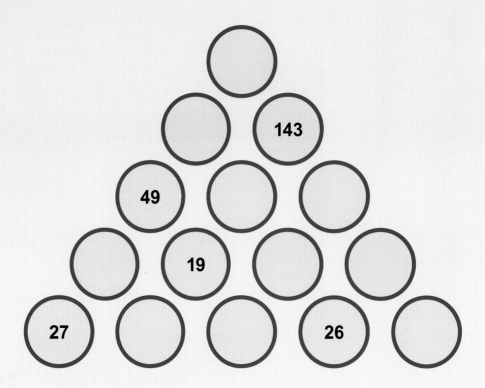

Making Arrangements

Arrange one each of the four numbers below, as well as one each of the symbols x (times), – (minus), and + (plus) in every row and column. You should arrive at the answer at the end of the row or column, making the calculations in the order in which they appear. Some are already in place. Write your answers on a separate sheet of paper.

Circling In

The three empty circles should contain the symbols +, − , and x in some order, to make a series that leads to the number in the middle. Each symbol must be used once and calculations are made in a clockwise direction. Write your answers on a separate sheet of paper.

=

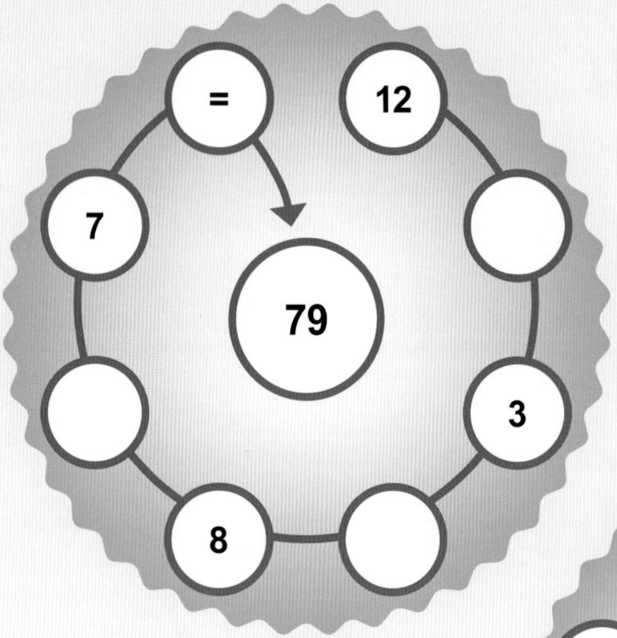

12

7

79

3

8

=

18

4

132

13

28

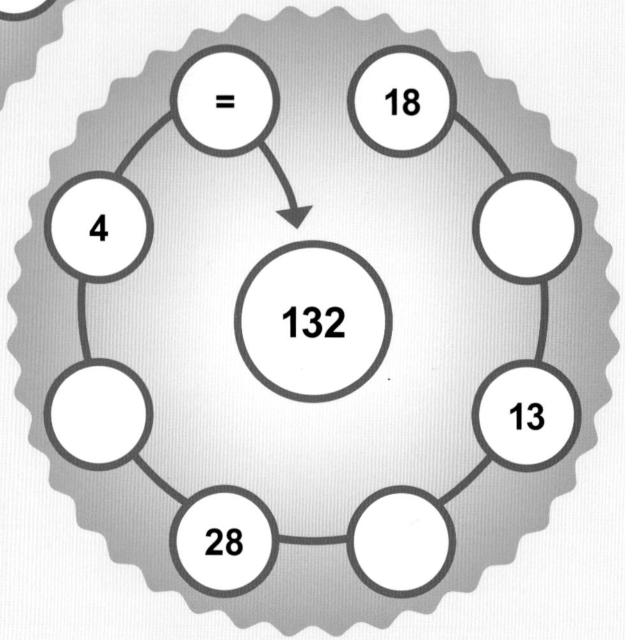

Symbol Math

Each symbol stands for a different number. In order to reach the correct total at the end of each row and column, what is the value of the circle, cross, pentagon, square, and star? Write your answers on a separate sheet of paper.

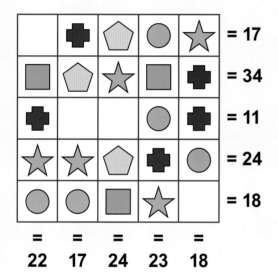

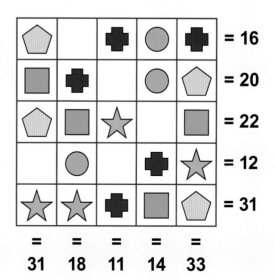

What's the Number?

In the diagram below, what number should replace the question mark?
Write your answer on a separate sheet of paper.

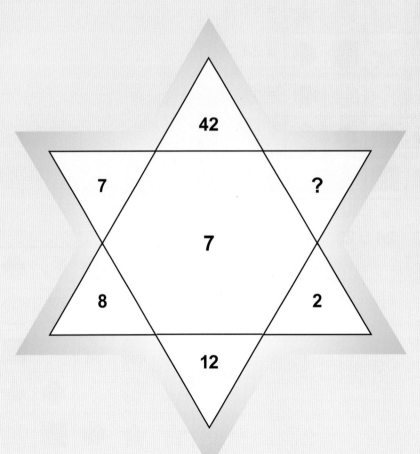

Pyramid Plus

The number in each circle is the sum of the two numbers below it. Just work out the missing numbers in every circle! Write your answers on a separate sheet of paper.

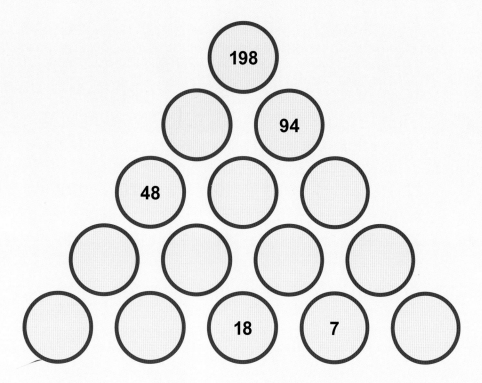

Total Concentration

The blank squares below should contain whole numbers between 1 and 30 inclusive, any of which may occur more than once, or not at all. The numbers in every horizontal row add up to the totals on the right, as do the two long diagonal lines extending from corner to corner; those in every vertical column add up to the totals along the bottom. Write your answers on a separate sheet of paper.

							147
12	18		22	5		21	115
	28	14	13		30		121
22		4	21	16	13	20	120
29	15			11	20	26	136
29		17	18	26		16	119
	19	19		2	24	28	134
	9	27	25		25		119
127	116	112	156	98	136	119	122

One to Nine

Using the numbers one to nine, complete these six equations (three reading across and three reading downward). Every number is used once only, and one is already in place. Write your answers on a separate sheet of paper.

22

1 2 3 4 5 6 7 8 9

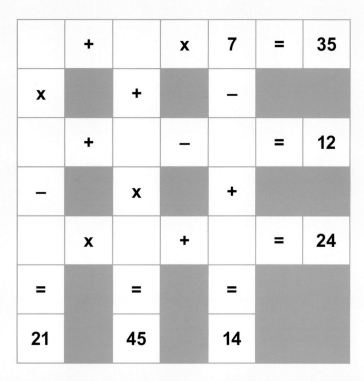

	+		x	7	=	35
x		+		−		
	+		−		=	12
−		x		+		
	x		+		=	24
=		=		=		
21		45		14		

Circling In

The three empty circles should contain the symbols +, − , and x in some order, to make a series that leads to the number in the middle. Each symbol must be used once and calculations are made in a clockwise direction. Write your answers on a separate sheet of paper.

23

24

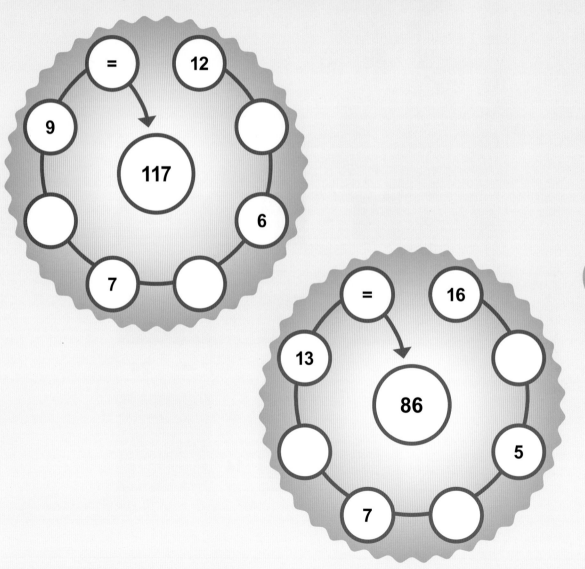

What's the Number?

In the diagram below, what number should replace the question mark?
Write your answer on a separate sheet of paper.

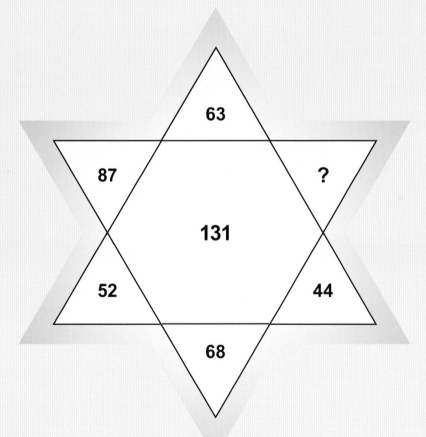

Number Crunch

Starting at the top left with the number provided, work down from one box to another, applying the mathematical instructions to your running total. Write your answers on a separate sheet of paper.

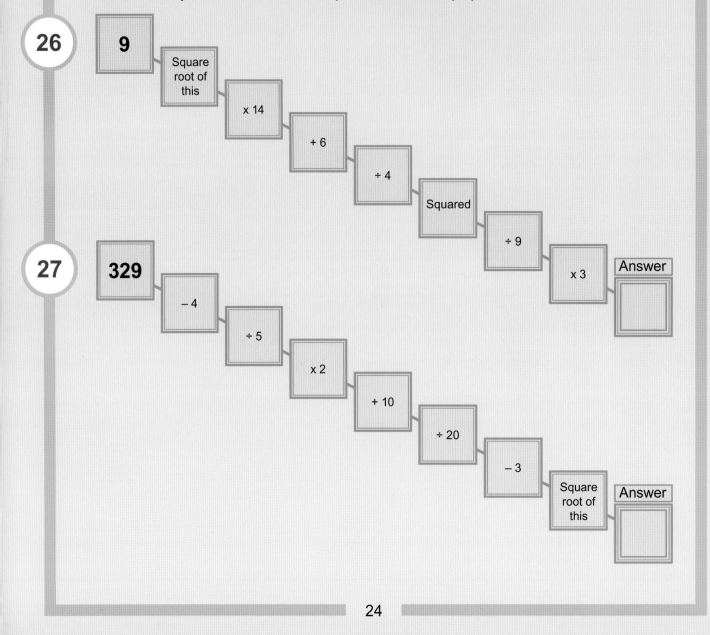

26

9 → Square root of this → x 14 → + 6 → ÷ 4 → Squared → ÷ 9 → x 3 → Answer

27

329 → − 4 → ÷ 5 → x 2 → + 10 → ÷ 20 → − 3 → Square root of this → Answer

One to Nine

Using the numbers one to nine, complete these six equations (three reading across and three reading downward). Every number is used once only, and one is already in place. Write your answers on a separate sheet of paper.

1 2 3 4 5 6 7 8 9

	+		x		=	10
x		−		+		
	−		x		=	9
+		x		x		
	x	4	+		=	34
=		=		=		
26		8		20		

Circling In

The three empty circles should contain the symbols +, – , and x in some order, to make a series that leads to the number in the middle. Each symbol must be used once and calculations are made in a clockwise direction. Write your answers on a separate sheet of paper.

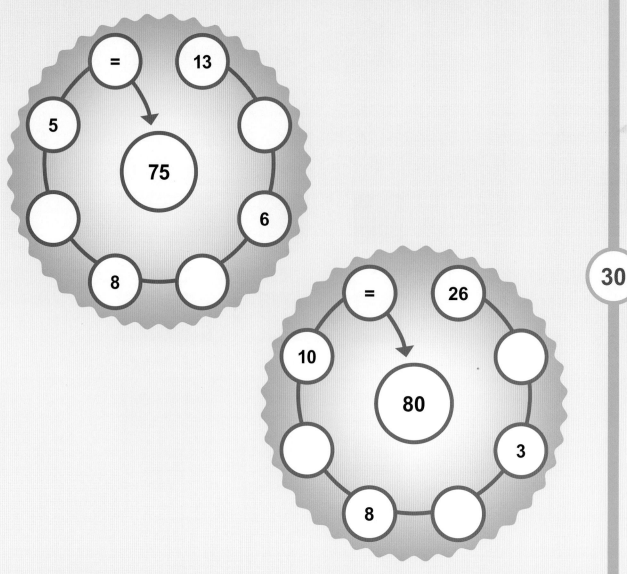

One to Nine

Using the numbers one to nine, complete these six equations (three reading across and three reading downward). Every number is used once only, and one is already in place. Write your answers on a separate sheet of paper.

1 2 3 4 5 6 7 8 9

	x		–	9	=	9
+		–		+		
	+		x		=	49
x		x		x		
	–		+		=	11
=		=		=		
40		1		64		

Number Crunch

Starting at the top left with the number provided, work down from one box to another, applying the mathematical instructions to your running total. Write your answers on a separate sheet of paper.

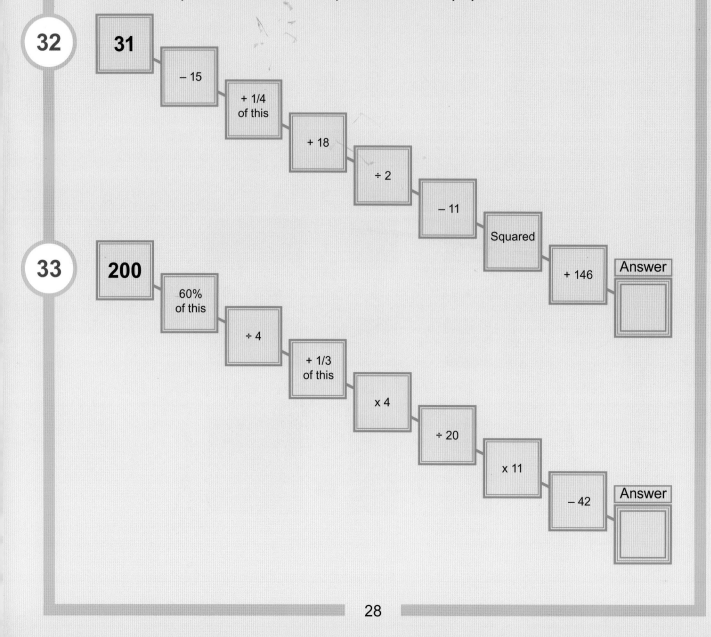

32

31
− 15
+ 1/4 of this
+ 18
÷ 2
− 11
Squared
+ 146
Answer

33

200
60% of this
÷ 4
+ 1/3 of this
x 4
÷ 20
x 11
− 42
Answer

Circling In

The three empty circles should contain the symbols +, – , and x in some order, to make a series that leads to the number in the middle. Each symbol must be used once and calculations are made in a clockwise direction. Write your answers on a separate sheet of paper.

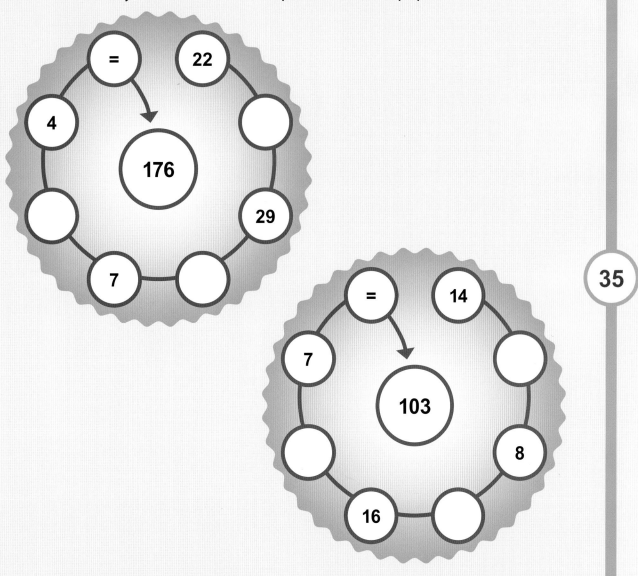

Pyramid Plus

The number in each circle is the sum of the two numbers below it. Just work out the missing numbers in every circle! Write your answers on a separate sheet of paper.

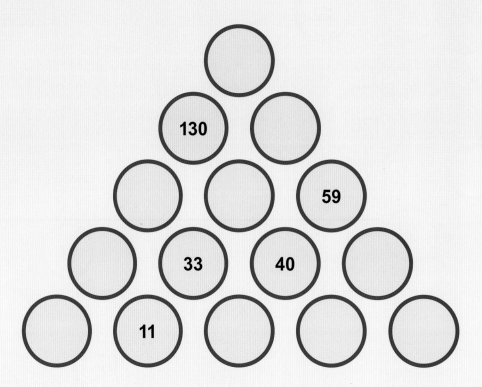

Total Concentration

The blank squares below should contain whole numbers between 1 and 30 inclusive, any of which may occur more than once, or not at all. The numbers in every horizontal row add up to the totals on the right, as do the two long diagonal lines extending from corner to corner; those in every vertical column add up to the totals along the bottom. Write your answers on a separate sheet of paper.

							87
	5	4	5	18	28		120
21	21	23			4	24	137
27	6	17		3		9	110
	26	20	3	24	10		101
14		25	19	11		1	112
29	2		19		8	23	123
		1	18	28	27		114
143	98	102	119	129	116	110	97

31

What's the Number?

In the diagram below, what number should replace the question mark? Write your answer on a separate sheet of paper.

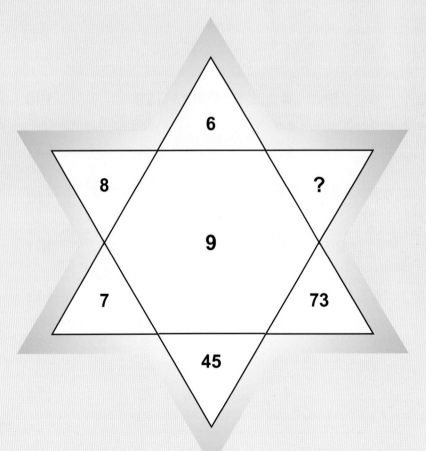

Circling In

The three empty circles should contain the symbols +, − , and x in some order, to make a series that leads to the number in the middle. Each symbol must be used once and calculations are made in a clockwise direction. Write your answers on a separate sheet of paper.

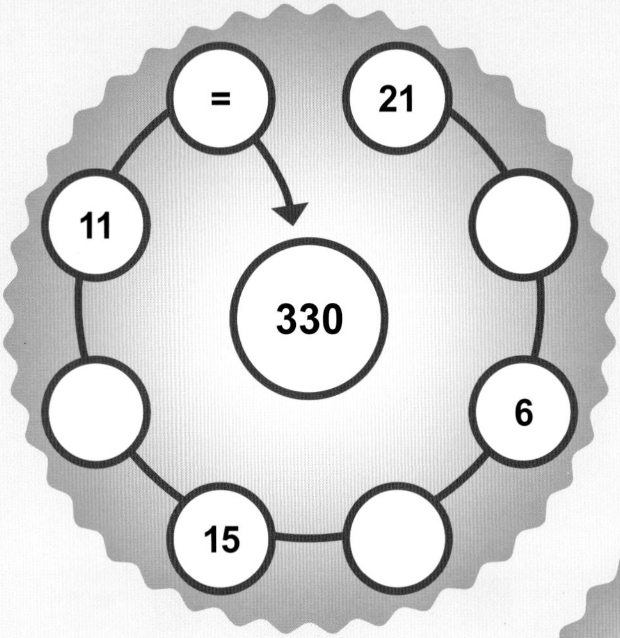

=
21
11
330
6
15

=
18
6
126
7
4

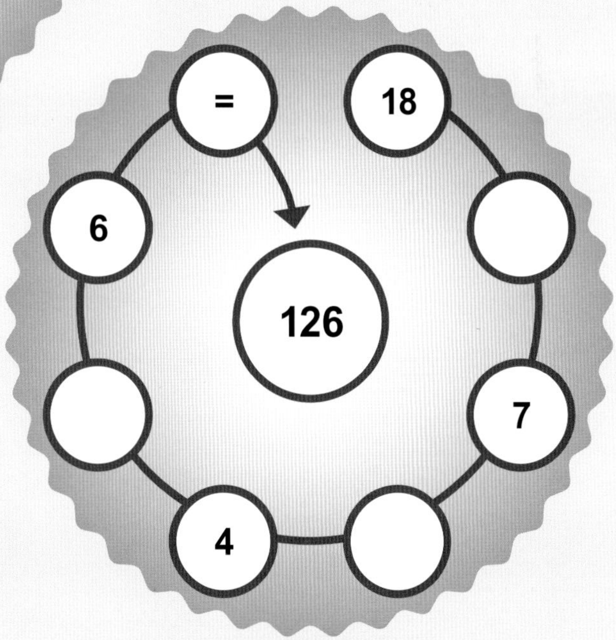

Symbol Math

Each symbol stands for a different number. In order to reach the correct total at the end of each row and column, what is the value of the circle, pentagon, square, and star? Write your answers on a separate sheet of paper.

41

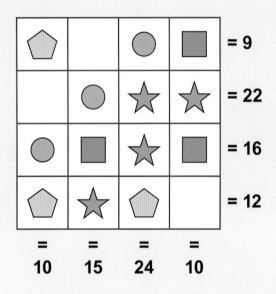

42

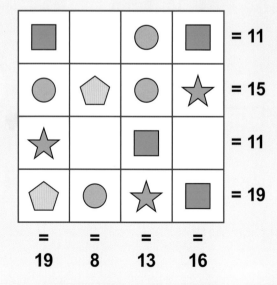

34

Pyramid Plus

The number in each circle is the sum of the two numbers below it. Just work out the missing numbers in every circle! Write your answers on a separate sheet of paper.

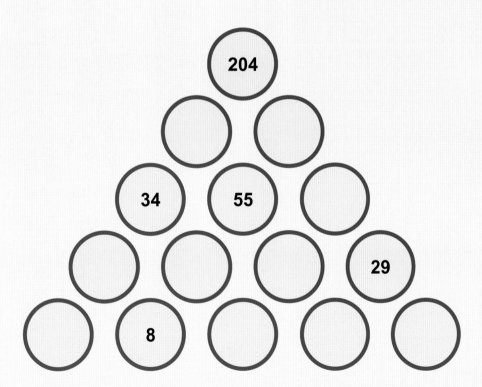

Total Concentration

44

The blank squares below should contain whole numbers between 1 and 30 inclusive, any of which may occur more than once, or not at all. The numbers in every horizontal row add up to the totals on the right, as do the two long diagonal lines extending from corner to corner; those in every vertical column add up to the totals along the bottom. Write your answers on a separate sheet of paper.

							121

20	1	22		1		21	**101**
23			15	24	17	30	**126**
3		13	16		6	21	**98**
12			5	14	29		**139**
	4	11	26	26		7	**111**
29	25	18			28	18	**155**
19	10	27	2		8		**112**
123	**101**	**117**	**87**	**135**	**130**	**149**	**134**

Making Arrangements

Arrange one each of the four numbers below, as well as one each of the symbols x (times), – (minus), and + (plus) in every row and column. You should arrive at the answer at the end of the row or column, making the calculations in the order in which they appear. Some are already in place. Write your answers on a separate sheet of paper.

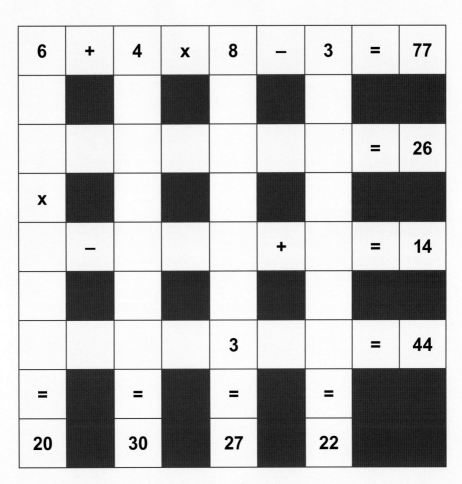

Number Crunch

Starting at the top left with the number provided, work down from one box to another, applying the mathematical instructions to your running total. Write your answers on a separate sheet of paper.

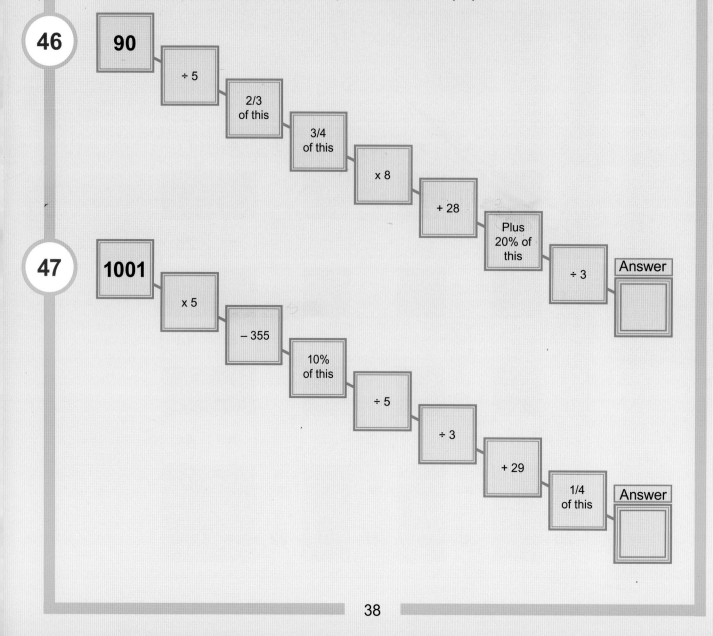

46

90 → ÷ 5 → 2/3 of this → 3/4 of this → x 8 → + 28 → Plus 20% of this → ÷ 3 → Answer

47

1001 → x 5 → − 355 → 10% of this → ÷ 5 → ÷ 3 → + 29 → 1/4 of this → Answer

Word Puzzles

48

Running Time
The world record for running a marathon is 2:03:59. The Boston Marathon starts at 10 AM local time, but the live TV coverage begins 90 minutes into the race. At what time should people in San Francisco turn on their televisions, if Pacific Time is three hours behind Eastern?

49

Setting the Alarm
Sarah needs to be at school at 8:15 AM. If it takes her 20 minutes to shower and get dressed, 15 minutes to eat, and 25 minutes to walk to school, what time should she get up?

50

Matching Up
The Men's and Women's singles event at the US Open tennis tournament each begins with 128 players. In round one, each player has one match and the losers are out of the tournament. In round two, half of that total is eliminated in the same way, and so on until only two players remain in each event (competing in the Final). At the end of the tournament, how many singles matches were played—men's and women's?

1

4	x	6	−	9	=	15
+		x		+		
8	−	1	x	3	=	21
−		+		x		
2	x	5	+	7	=	17
=		=		=		
10		11		84		

2

3	+	8	x	2	−	7	=	15
−		−		+		+		
2	+	7	−	3	x	8	=	48
+		+		x		x		
7	−	3	+	8	x	2	=	24
x		x		−		−		
8	x	2	−	7	+	3	=	12
=		=		=		=		
64		8		33		27		

3

66 – Starting at the top and working clockwise, 12 + 3 = 15 x 2 = 30 + 3 = 33 x 2 = 66 + 3 = 69 x 2 = 138.

4

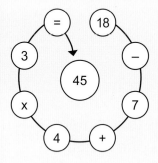

5

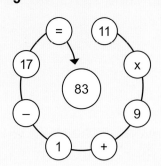

6

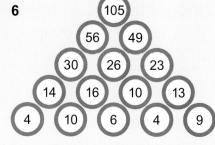

7

8	−	6	x	4	=	8
+		x		+		
1	+	3	x	9	=	36
x		+		x		
5	x	7	−	2	=	33
=		=		=		
45		25		26		

8

							119
22	30	1	18	23	6	21	121
24	12	20	27	16	24	15	138
7	17	22	11	3	20	30	110
23	4	29	17	28	9	22	132
25	1	16	2	29	28	26	127
8	26	14	18	25	10	27	128
12	13	19	11	5	19	21	100
121	103	121	104	129	116	162	133

9

Circle = 3, Pentagon = 4, Square = 5, Star = 9.

10

Circle = 1, Pentagon = 7, Square = 8, Star = 6.

11

13² = 169, 169 + 31 = 200, 200 ÷ 4 = 50, 50 x 5 = 250, 250 + 25 = 275, 275 − 125 = 150, 150 ÷ 3 = 50

12

59 − 26 = 33, 33 ÷ 11 = 3, 3 x 7 = 21, 21 + 14 = 35, 35 + 7 = 42, 42 ÷ 6 = 7, 7 x 4 = 28

13

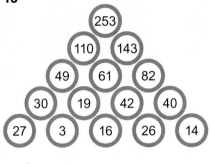

14

5	−	3	+	8	x	7	=	70
+		x		−		+		
8	+	7	−	5	x	3	=	30
x		−		x		−		
3	x	8	+	7	−	5	=	26
−		+		+		x		
7	−	5	x	3	+	8	=	14
=		=		=		=		
32		18		24		40		

15

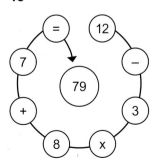

16

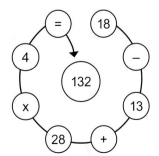

17

Circle = 1, Cross = 5, Pentagon = 4, Square = 9, Star = 7.

18

Circle = 3, Cross = 2, Pentagon = 9, Square = 6, Star = 7.

19

28 – In opposite points of the star, the lower number is multiplied by the central number and the result is divided by two to equal the higher number, so 8 x 7 = 56 divided by two = 28.

20

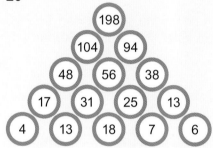

21

							147
12	18	23	22	5	14	21	115
6	28	14	13	23	30	7	121
22	24	4	21	16	13	20	120
29	15	8	27	11	20	26	136
29	3	17	18	26	10	16	119
12	19	19	30	2	24	28	134
17	9	27	25	15	25	1	119
127	116	112	156	98	136	119	122

22

4	+	1	x	7	=	35
x		+		−		
6	+	8	−	2	=	12
−		x		+		
3	x	5	+	9	=	24
=		=		=		
21		45		14		

23

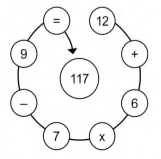

24

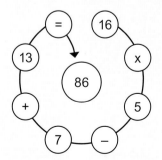

25

79 – The numbers on opposite points of the star total the number in the middle.

26

Square root of 9 = 3, 3 x 14 = 42, 42 + 6 = 48, 48 ÷ 4 = 12, 12^2 = 144, 144 ÷ 9 = 16, 16 x 3 = 48

27

329 – 4 = 325, 325 ÷ 5 = 65, 65 x 2 = 130, 130 + 10 = 140, 140 ÷ 20 = 7, 7 – 3 = 4, square root of 4 = 2

28

3	+	7	x	1	=	10
x		–		+		
6	–	5	x	9	=	9
+		x		x		
8	x	4	+	2	=	34
=		=		=		
26		8		20		

29

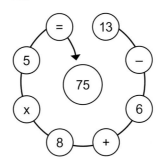

30

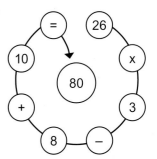

31

3	x	6	–	9	=	9
+		–		+		
2	+	5	x	7	=	49
x		x		x		
8	–	1	+	4	=	11
=		=		=		
40		1		64		

32

31 – 15 = 16, 16 + 4 = 20, 20 + 18 = 38, 38 ÷ 2 = 19, 19 – 11 = 8, 8^2 = 64, 64 + 146 = 210

33

60% of 200 = 120, 120 ÷ 4 = 30, 30 + 10 = 40, 40 x 4 = 160, 160 ÷ 20 = 8, 8 x 11 = 88, 88 – 42 = 46

34

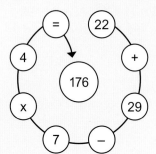

35

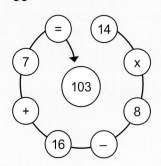

36

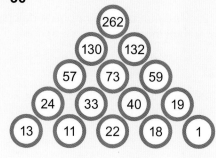

37

87

30	5	4	5	18	28	30	120
21	21	23	29	15	4	24	137
27	6	17	26	3	22	9	110
2	26	20	3	24	10	16	101
14	25	25	19	11	17	1	112
29	2	12	19	30	8	23	123
20	13	1	18	28	27	7	114

143	98	102	119	129	116	110	97

38

58 – Each single-digit number is squared and the result is added to the central number to give the number in the opposite point of the star.

39

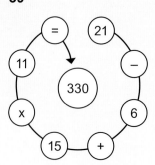

40

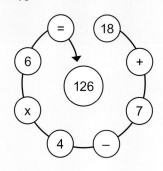

41

Circle = 6, Pentagon = 2, Square = 1, Star = 8.

42

Circle = 1, Pentagon = 7, Square = 5, Star = 6.

43

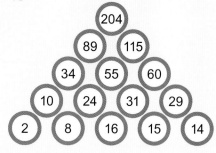

44

							121
20	1	22	14	1	22	21	101
23	15	2	15	24	17	30	126
3	16	13	16	23	6	21	98
12	30	24	5	14	29	25	139
17	4	11	26	26	20	7	111
29	25	18	9	28	28	18	155
19	10	27	2	19	8	27	112
123	101	117	87	135	130	149	134

45

6	+	4	x	8	−	3	=	77
−		+		−		x		
3	x	8	−	4	+	6	=	26
x		x		x		+		
4	−	3	x	6	+	8	=	14
+		−		+		−		
8	+	6	−	3	x	4	=	44
=		=		=		=		
20		30		27		22		

46

90 ÷ 5 = 18, 18 ÷ 3 x 2 = 12, 12 ÷ 4 x 3 = 9,
9 x 8 = 72, 72 + 28 = 100, 100 + 20 = 120,
120 ÷ 3 = 40

47

1001 x 5 = 5005, 5005 − 355 = 4650, 10%
of 4650 = 465, 465 ÷ 5 = 93, 93 ÷ 3 = 31,
31 + 29 = 60, 60 ÷ 4 = 15

48

8:30 AM

49

7:15 AM

50

254 (127 men's and 127 women's)

Glossary

calculation   The use of math to find a solution.

clockwise   A circular movement that goes in the same direction that a clock's hands travel.

column   A line of objects that goes straight up and down.

concentration   Thinking very hard and examining every possibility.

diagonal   Moving in a slanted direction, halfway between straight across and straight down.

diagram   A drawing or outline to explain how something works.

horizontal   A direction that is straight across.

inclusive   Including both ends of a series (two to five inclusive means 2, 3, 4, and 5).

occur   To happen.

pentagon   A five-sided object.

pyramid   A triangular shape with one side level to the ground and a point at the top.

row   A line of objects that goes straight across.

square root   A number that, if multiplied by itself, produces the original number (3 is the square root of 9; 4 is the square root of 16).

squared   When a number is multiplied by itself (3 squared = 3 x 3 = 9).

symbol   An image that represents something else.

vertical   A direction that is straight up and down.

whole number   A number that has no decimals (4 is a whole number; 4.3 is not a whole number).

Further Information

For More Information

Consortium for Mathematics (COMAP)
175 Middlesex Turnpike, Bedford, MA 01730
(800) 772-6627 http://www.comap.com/index.html
COMAP is a nonprofit organization whose mission is to improve mathematics education for students of all ages. It works with teachers, students, and business people to create learning environments where mathematics is used to investigate and model real issues in our world.

MATHCOUNTS Foundation
1420 King Street, Alexandria, VA 22314
(703) 299-9006 https://mathcounts.org/sslpage.aspx
MATHCOUNTS is a national enrichment, club, and competition program that promotes middle school mathematics achievement. To secure America's global competitiveness, MATHCOUNTS inspires excellence, confidence, and curiosity in U.S. middle school students through fun and challenging math programs.

National Council of Teachers of Mathematics (NCTM)
906 Association Drive, Reston, VA 20191-1502
(703) 620-9840 http://www.nctm.org
The NCTM is a public voice of mathematics education supporting teachers to ensure equitable mathematics learning of the highest quality for all students through vision, leadership, professional development, and research.

Web Sites

Due to the changing nature of Internet links, Rosen Publishing has developed an online list of Web sites related to the subject of this book. This site is updated regularly. Please use this link to access this list:

http://www.rosenlinks.com/msw/comp

Further Reading

Abramson, Marcie F. *Painless Math Word Problems.* New York, NY: Barron's Educational Series, 2010.

Ball, Johnny. *Why Pi?* New York, NY: Dorling Kindersley, 2009.

Fisher, Richard W. *Mastering Essential Math Skills: Pre-Algebra Concepts: 20 Minutes a Day to Success.* Los Gatos, CA: Math Essentials, 2008.

Fisher, Richard W. *Mastering Essential Math Skills: 20 Minutes a Day to Success (Book Two: Middle Grades/High School).* Los Gatos, CA: Math Essentials, 2007.

Shortz, Will et al. *I Can KenKen! 75 Puzzles for Having Fun with Math.* New York, NY: St. Martin's Griffin, 2008.

Index